Collecting Life

Frances Daggar Roberts

Collecting Life

Dedicated to my parents Irene and Ken Daggar
and my brother Tony.
Thank you for always encouraging me to write.

Collecting Life
ISBN 978 1 76109 597 9
Copyright © text Frances Daggar Roberts 2022
Cover image: Frances Daggar Roberts

First published 2022 by
Ginninderra Press
PO Box 3461 Port Adelaide 5015
www.ginninderrapress.com.au

Contents

1

Threshold	9
Newspapers	10
Love and Fury	12
Owl Watching	13
Regret	15
Moonflower	16

2

San Vitale Ravenna	19
Farewell Old Zia	20
Syracuse – Fountain of Arethusa	21
Intimates	22
Meeting the Day	23
Alive	24
End of the day	25
Goodbye	26
Bare Heart	27
To a Sea Nymph's Love	28
A Given	29

3

Peter's Hands	33
Three Stages	34
Reminiscence	35
Twined	36
Star fish	37
Last Skier	38
Contempt	39
Sylvan	40
Creek Daring	42

The Smell of Place	43
The Aunts	44

4

Forgetting	47
A New Language	48
Day's End	49
News of an Imminent Death	50
Afternoon Tea	51
Approaching ACT	52
Sam Mantis	53
A Reluctant Farewell	54

5

Albedo	57
Day's End	58
Love in Winter	59
Parting	60
For Micki	61
Flight of Words	62
Spirit dawn	63
Building Children	64
Another Blood Red Sunrise	65
My Old Friend	66
Salute to Poetry	67

1

Threshold

Under a pale moon,
we sat upon my father's boat
and dreamed.
Quiet water lapped
against the hull,
mysteriously dark
as futures.

Newspapers

Our father brought them from the office
and read them at night beside the fire
or on the weekends in the sitting room
while the afternoon grew long with shadows.

They fuelled discussions and instruction
the iniquities of the world brought to our bushland home
a transport of astounding happenings:
Ben Chifley replaced by Menzies at election
the polio epidemic crippling other people's children
progress on the Snowy Mountains Scheme
the road death of a child like us – a cautionary tale.

We watched the flames that started with old crumpled pages
sometimes wreathed in turpentine
used to clean paintbrushes or to wipe down creosote
blue spurts flaring among the logs and sticks.

Then there were the garden beds beside the house
mysteriously laid sheets of earth and paper
excluding weeds retaining moisture
boosting our love of strawberries
which we christened paperberries
and on an indoors rainy day papier-mâché sculptures
that might wrench the face of Rodin into a grimace.

But the finest application of the papers
was the ride down to our 'tip'
crushed tight against my brother side by side
on the front edge of a barrow full of garbage
our perch laid thick with news sheets to protect our jeans...
rollicking songs and squeals of fear – a circus ride.

Love and Fury

I remember the kicking well
the extraordinary desire to dismember him
when he hit the sweet spot on my knee.
It set our mother flapping arms and tea towels –
'stop that now – you know it will end in tears!'
Of course it would that was the point.
When I was ten and he was eight I had the reach
but then I was a skinny teen
and he was a sturdy twelve and held me down.

The grandchildren do it now –
from loving teasing laughter
to fierce battle within seconds…
Inevitably an enlistment of parental justice
and then like puppies wound together
they roll and fall from the back of the lounge
into the cushions to begin again.
Is it thus we learn
the rules of war and marriage?

Owl Watching

I never knew her, my father's mother.
I met her once or twice that I remember
the last occasion being
in the week in which she died
when I was afraid
but ushered in to take her hand
and say something
beside her canopied bed.

After she died
I wondered if she used to cuddle me
when I was plump and wordless,
easily smiling
without a head brimful
of questions.

I remember going to her house
and standing solemn
in the billiard room
while the men played there.
My place was near the doorway
by the bell jar with its occupant
a large brown owl
with empty eyes.

So many questions answered
but never what was in my heart.
How did it die? Did you love it?
They fobbed me off with tales
of owl night vision…
Puzzled they watched me
seek it out to stand
and stare into its face.

It was a silent communication
of some sort…
the billiard room, that bird,
the image of her bed
enclosed by drapes,
are all I have of her.

Regret

Steeped in high spirits
the boys unfurled laughter
and swung it about
tripping one another.

The small group surged forward
like a single mayhem unit
and rushed on the sleepy cat
beside the garden fence.

Startled to its feet
it fled along the fence line
under the pickets
and out into the street.

They shouted war cries
storming forward in pursuit
as neighbours backed from a driveway
and struck the small grey form.

The group stood still in shock…
one child gently lifted the ruin of the cat
saw the fragile tongue extruded
and sobbed for the end of its world.

Moonflower

Epiphylum Oxipetalum

Under a dazzling moon an intricate star unfolds
releasing threads of perfume
to lace the darker spaces with desire
casting olfactory nets
lures prompts…
to bumbling insects
and to human hearts.

Awe-filled   in silent worship
we savour the brief perfection
never to stand in a vase and wilt
closing with moon's ebbing light
in a deity's white death
secret beauty left to bloom
inside the mind an exquisite mystery.

2

San Vitale Ravenna

Men with strong hands and short lives
religious brothers lit from within
hardworking visionaries
put together the faces of their dreams.

Against the odds their work remains
and resonates with us
more than fifteen hundred years
beyond their impassioned sight.

Here in an urban summer
they could never even have imagined
upon their skins
I gaze into the faces of their saints.

The sad eyes of their convictions
look back at me
and provoke a tenderness
as gentle as sorrow's kiss.

Farewell Old Zia

Zia Maria's bony fluttering hands
are as compelling as her strange deep voice.
She is a tiny fragile butterfly woman
with an oxygen cylinder behind the couch
in ominous stand-by.
We bring our news and clumsy cheer
and wrestle with the holes left by her dialect.
Her carer brings us tea and the faltering
kind assistance of Ukrainian English.
A little piece of the afternoon stands still
as we offer Zia bite-sized bits of tenderness
to make her smile
but tears shine in her eyes because she knows
we will not meet again.

Syracuse – Fountain of Arethusa

Most places separate daily life
from concepts of a life of spirits
but this location blends the two
uniquely plaited like papyrus strands
fibre to fibre   dream to reality –
revelations of the past coiled in the present.

Huge ancient stones are used as seats
or in rowdy children's jumping games.
Lovers stare into the water's murky depths
where others stood unmapped years before.
The locals quote the legend of the nymph
as though she might appear at any moment
from between the rushes.

Intimates

They were casually hung to dry
with shirts and socks upon a windowsill
above the passers-by
at least that was until the wind
snatched up the cheeky piece
but left the others dangling.
Peering down we saw the item
the tell-tale edge against the wall
of black stripes and silky lace…
But what to do?
Go down and claim lost underwear
in the passeggiata hours?
Claim it as something lost in shame
or a trophy fancied just in passing?
We chose the prudence of recovery in the dark
but when in the night we sought the item out
it was no longer there…
We see it now as a fitting end.
It was well worn and loved
but aged beyond its best.
What better way to end it all
than whisked from a fancy balcony
over the bay of Syracuse
to float down in glowing light
and disappear.

Meeting the Day

Sun on my back and the emerging day
is shedding its night wraps
newspapers and iPhones at all the tables.
An early yawning quiet holds sway.
I savour the sugar on my coffee's froth

but just outside the café on the street corner
I see a man with a shaved head.
He unties a bedroll to sit there
slightly crumpled beside a mug.
The sun does not quite reach his legs.

Alive

A tribute to Schopenhauer's 'When you die you return to what you were before you were born'

Are you afraid of the darkness
around the corner
of the end of light and thought
or do you see the improbable
gift of consciousness
as a constant celebration
a moment's window on existence –
a miracle of perception
between silences.

End of the day

I cut you with a statement
about when I must go home
and I feel your pain beside me
as we lie in silence.
The day's potential dims
though nothing changes
in the light outside.
You offer me a wound
in return for yours
and my silence flows into yours
like a dark tide.

Goodbye

Such tears inside sweet fruit
staining the heart.
The scent of you has lingered
masking reception
from all other senses
a sweetness of perpetual sorrow.

Bare Heart

What shall I play or dance or write
without the muse who filled my thought
with metaphors of fire and light,
inspiring all the ways I sought
to fashion visions of this life –
visions to lift hearts from the strife
of battles, losses, pain and grief
and offer moments of relief?

She gave me a sense of competence,
of honour in artistic striving,
of joy to see a skill reviving,
regardless of the world's events.
Bereft of her, my dreams now wither
and drift stick grey on sorrow's river.

To a Sea Nymph's Love

Not for the first time
my heart flies to you,
over the sand
and the curled wave's spume,
through crevices
and beach rock erosions,
over stoic clinging banksias
and the rowdy complaints of seagulls,
into the warm sweet harbour
of your welcome.

A Given

The field where we courted was small and green
enclosed by a school and the backyards of houses.
In that field I set my flag –
and so you fell to me as I to you.
We lived surrounded by my children
in a place of all things green.

Back then, did you fear the undertow?
Did you see the bank it cut between the two of us?
Did you guess the tide would rush inshore
and swallow all we knew
that this bleak season would erode
memories and hopes alike?

I never guessed I would betray
the kindness we once thought an axiom –
the laughter and the promises all swept away.
It took me by surprise
as a birth cuts child from mother
as death cuts time.

And yet your constant tender thought
and ever sunny heart
have borne me on a different tide
beyond the shame and doubt
to the certainty of something
transfiguring all.

Evergreen loving welcomes this wayfarer's steps
with food and kindness, patience and forgiveness.

3

Peter's Hands

He speaks,
and moves his hands in punctuation
along the outlines of his words
along the sliprail fence
along the surface of his axe
the stroke of truth.

The dogs,
cognisant of the love beneath the touch
accept the callused kindness tossed
as if by accident
brusquely fond against their muzzles
work mates' pact.

An owl,
whose blundered flight impaled it
is deftly plucked from thorns and freed
by gipsy craft
horse-dealer's knowledge flashing
sleight of hand.
In movement,

A sureness that betrays the lover underlying
dark with passion and with ownership…
my tender dear whose hard work hands
hold myth of land secure
within a rough caress.

Three Stages

Her tiny fingers curled
reflexly around mine
bonding as a little ape
clutching my heart to hers.

Crossing the road I snatched her hand
a wild grab to keep her safe
accepted with a guilty laugh
and toss of hair.

Today it was her
linking my arm in the rain
her strong hands wrapping me
against the risks of slippery paving.

Reminiscence

He and I talk as always
tangled in threads of memories.
Tears are shared for a lost love of long ago
a beauty that stole the weather from the day.
Outside a small surrender of rain
gathers in heavier drops
on the ledge above the window.
Each droplet pauses swells and strikes
the grapevine underneath.
This audible gravity strangely echoes
the old man's ponderous choice of words
from his handsome outmoded vocabulary.
He and I both note the slow selection
of each verbal jewel.
We meet each other's eye as we register the sound.
The smile erases years.

Twined

I thought it was the sun upon our days –
The bright light across the water and the snow
while we skied and rode the wind and laughed.
It was instead the seam of gold in you –
the honey coloured kindness of your being
that declared itself like morning.

I didn't realise the treasure that you threaded
through our days –
the vein of joyfulness
a forgiving, resilient happiness
that was never more than a touch away
on the dark surface of our time.

Star fish

In those big seas many things were tangled
and abandoned on the sand

at my feet a small mauve starfish squirmed slightly
thrown from the night sky onto a desert

I washed it free of sand and carried it
to the rock platform

a life of inconsequence in the natural world
in the hand of a life of inconsequence in the universe

and yet in its new deep rock pool perhaps it will find a mate
and will creep in flickering light contented with its lot

a grain of life among the bigger grains of earthly life
among celestial grains out here on Orion's spiral arm .

Last Skier

A low sun flares across the top of the slope.
The rocks are growing huge dark wings.
I too have wings that flap behind me
as I crest the final icy rise
above the evening valley.
Down there it is blue as woodsmoke,
indistinct as a watermark,
but here the air glows gold
and I swoop through shimmering light
above enchanted fields.
On these wings I ride through dreams
for a few more shining moments,
before the plummeting descent
into the twilight.

Contempt

My brother made moves
to foil the possums
his efforts insubstantial
but elegant as a shoji screen.
The possum bully boys
obdurate and confident
ignored his installation
scattered faeces contemptuously
smashed their way through
to their ceiling hideout.

Sylvan

A childhood in wild countryside –
what a legacy that upbringing!
I took it all for granted
until now.

Here among a population
from a high-rise world
I see a fear in confrontation
with the bushland –

with small creatures who are
our other selves and teach
not only coping but exhilaration
for our place within the chain of life.

They activate a biological wisdom
that makes us secure and whole
acknowledging our interdependence
and the role of differences.

I wish I had charisma
sufficient to be a champion
for these true god-spirits
of the earth.

for I see them eradicated
struck down by speeding cars
their food trees cut
their access blocked…

Their retreating calls
implore an escort for them
from the built world to a place
beyond the reach of human taint.

Creek Daring

There was a place
where the creek narrowed suddenly
to thrust through a rocky channel
before fanning out in bridal lace
and tumbling to the pool below.

To stand there in the channel
hands tight in the crevices
braced against the pull
was a sensual game
of dominance and defiance.

Withdrawing was the biggest challenge –
the risk of losing traction
of rock scrapes and spiky arms of epacris
with no protection but a singlet
thin and almost always torn.

There is a laughter in such places
unknown to those who only know
the urban world
a merriment that rises from the sanctuary of a pool
and interlocks with birdsong.

The Smell of Place

A wisp of spice as dry as nutmeg
coachwood in the still hot air –
and under that the darker fruity smell
of loamy earth and lichen.
A few steps further down the slope
and paperbark's damp mustiness
proclaims the brackish waterway nearby.
Crushed leaves beneath my feet
exude the sharp bright smell of turpentine
perverse reflection of development
upon the ridge above.

I long for scent alone to lead me
though it's not an overlay of city fumes
that robs me of olfactory palette
but limitations of acuity…

we only can discriminate
what is experienced
and rarely now do townsfolk
follow trails upon the air.
Along with forest shrinkage
comes withering of capacity to smell.
That deep-brain knowledge of our ancient world
is dimming as we lose the time
the heart and interest to identify by nose.
And so it is these piquant vivid landscapes
must shrink and fade around us.

The Aunts

Relatives by marriage
one deaf one almost blind
tottering through the dusk.
Their friendship grew
and roped them to each other
safe on any climb.
They understood and liked each other.
Out and about in the community
they made one whole and able being
crossing roads   buying goods
measuring the day's events…
a shared and tender confidence.

4

Forgetting

Words are escaping me like flights of butterflies
a departure of the beautiful and temporary occupants
of the libraries of my mind.

There are quiet places in those chambers –
reading rooms and contemplative spaces
where the erstwhile me still sits in tranquil rumination

but fewer of those chambers are in access now –
the entrance to the halls is hidden or the code denied me…
so many interesting annals I can no longer open

and yet on those rare occasions when I do
the names of things come fluttering back within my reach
and some I capture full of eager recognition.

A New Language

Nominal aphasia
names and faces blur
a social impediment
most certainly
but a different part of brain
comes into play
refines its leaps
its links and chains of words.
The stuff of metaphor
flourishes –
blooms like a magic garden
as the barriers of precision
are gloriously forgone.

Day's End

Suspended between two darks
that daily replica of our lifespan
I watch the early evening clouds
engulf a setting sun –
so beautiful a prelude
to the saturated black
of winter nightfall.
Can closure be like this
in the final years:
a heart steeped in gratitude
lit by colours more radiant
than those of childhood
or maybe even courtship
sliding softly into the dark.

News of an Imminent Death

I am walking a great deal
walking from room to room
locomotion to displace misery
or as a substitute for the fact
that I cannot go to his side.
It seems I cannot settle anywhere.

Could it be at times like this
we turn in part to an animal self
that once roamed perhaps for miles
into the comfort of old territory.
No one else is home here now
and I am glad of private space.

The anguish that his wife will feel
when his last breath is drawn
seems more normal
and more manageable
than this quiet foretaste
of the absence of my friend.

The earth that I believed so aptly tagged
'the green-blue planet'
is not as it appears.
It is in reality pitted with black holes
that suck my friends and family
into nothingness.

Afternoon Tea

Her knife words carried poison…
we could see his pallor
and his stiffened body
within seconds of each strike –
'Yes' he kept saying blankly.
She would have been a handsome girl
but mottled now by God knows what serpent change
she horrified – a Grecian gorgon.

I could not look away…
the red-rimmed glasses and the scarlet lips
the bright enamelled hair.
For want of other lifeline
I passed close by their table kicked his chair
just to meet his eye and smile
an apology for everything
in the corridors of pain we humans build.

Approaching ACT

A mournful landscape
skulking into evening.
The despoiling presence of humanity
is stark against the dusk:
a kangaroo carcass by the road
a plastic bag adrift
in home paddocks piles of oil drums and old tyres…
Can this really be the Federal Capital?
The road narrows.
The relief of a gorge
too deep to be frequented.
A rebellious froth of water
careens across the rocks.
Watching it cleans my mind.

Sam Mantis

Samson not Samuel…
strong square hands and perseverance
like his father – two things which serve to reconstruct
the beauty of his broken world.
Once they called him Mantis   long and thin he was
resembling his whittled men
when he walked the Western scrubland…
but Sam has diabetes now.
Thick fleshed he moves with effort
and the poetry in his carving costs him pain.
On market day the visitors stop for trifles
handle Sam's curious figures
buy some for their quaintness – a talking point upon a shelf.
No buyer sees the power they carry back to city life
or the prayer nets dragged behind Sam's men
the dream people   the caves   and trees
the dogs and roos and fish…
Bring them back the visions that once were
along with awe-filled worship
of those thousand white star nights
now faded out by glare from earth below.
When there is no star at all to see   perhaps no moon
Sam fears we will see nothing but ourselves.

A Reluctant Farewell

This night you were there but not there.
Time passed softly dragged like a branch across sand.
I remain held fast by memory of a special love
that defies analysis.
You have no particular beauty
your mind does not leap into the unknown
there is no fire of thought…
but when I think of you
I recognise something primeval
barbarously honest
older than the oceans
something emotionally genuine
that was there in the first light.
While we worked tonight you sat there
shawled in silence.
Wordless I sought connection with eyes and hands
willing songs of Circe to equip me
though constancy is an absurd notion
in a world in constant flux.
My head now fills
with the sad choreography
of farewells and isolation.

5

Albedo

White Queen, White Queen Albedo,
we've ignored you and your power
that role you've played in beaming heat
back into space.
All those long years of worshipping false gods
until we learned we might fare better
worshipping ourselves.
Labouring through those times of bombing
shooting   poisoning   we've reached a plateau
of complete control
where we can end it all without recourse
to costly weapons of any sort…
we can pursue the race for minerals
celebrity and power while the poor earth ends itself.
We can die without 'reflection'.
If on the brink of exit we decide
to hurtle into desperate response
and paint the brown earth white
perhaps we shall unleash another
tidal wave of horror as the ultimate hurrah.

Day's End

Suspended between two darks
that daily replica of our lifespan
I watch the early evening clouds
engulf a setting sun –
so beautiful a prelude
to the saturated black
of winter nightfall.
Can closure be like this
in the final years:
a heart steeped in gratitude
lit by colours more radiant
than those of childhood
or maybe even courtship
sliding softly into the dark.

Love in Winter

As we approach the lodge
the densely stippled air thins slightly
before the loaded snow-cat
eddies of fine flakes whirling upwards
to stick against struggling wipers.
My fingers hum with cold.

The baggage abandoned in the rooms
we curl into chairs and lounges beside the fire.
My son and his love sit discretely entwined.
It makes me think of jasmine in spring
small invisible tendrils reaching and joining
at every point that offers.

There is casual easy grace in the sprawl
of long young limbs.
A tenderness squeezes my heart
into the shape of times past.
The sadness of meeting perfection in existence
is the longing to shelter it forever from change.

Parting

The finality of going home
tears little tufts of sorrow
from the fabric of our meeting.
I blindly search among our moments
for the turns your mind has taken.
In hope of securing our connection
I offer you a keepsake penny
that travelled with me
down the years from childhood.

For Micki

Old friend old friend
who knew me with my hands
full of stars
and my heart blithe
how lovely now to fly
beyond our body forms
into a place resembling the past
but made of wisdom
kindness and of laughter –
the triumph of our well-lived lives.

Flight of Words

Lacking an address
I cast some swallow words
into the air.
Their northward swoop
along the coast
will catch your eye.
Plump with blessings
magenta bright against the sky
they sing of possibilities
beyond mere seeing.

Spirit dawn

The dawn beach is conjuring morning
from a menace of broiling cloud –
a magic lantern show of holes
and rapid changes.
Through one huge gleaming rent
my eagle heart sweeps skyward
to view this place below
where the tide around my feet
tugs gently at my anchor to the sand.
Earthbound only in part
I sing with the vast ocean's fugue
a hymn of thanks to the universe
for the exhilaration of a rising day
and the marvel of perception.

Building Children

We had two grandmothers – one rich and one poor.
The rich one did not like my mother or her origins
so we rarely saw her and always spoke
in stilted formulaic words
that made scratches on our hearts.

We saw the poor grandma each weekend
but called her aunty as her true identity
was masked by shame and packed away.
She and her sister cloaked us in belonging
celebrated cheered and challenged us.

Something of the safety and the wonder of that contact
set us to singing and to writing
building fantasies of words and possibilities
ethereal and uniquely strange as palaces beneath the sea.
How we wish we'd known the truth and thanked them.

Another Blood Red Sunrise

As the night grows round and heavy
before the new day's birth
bird calls make small ruptures in the dark
and the bloody stains across the tousled clouds
foretell the imminent child of mother time.

With all its beauty and seductive power
I mourn the harm it will deliver…
The cruel deeds that we will sanction in its name
assaults and heartless acts   desecrations of our land for profit
the loveliness sold out for political gain…
I keen the birth with those lamenters
of our previous days.

My Old Friend

How did we reach this place –
the years behind us fluttering like flags
above the journey outwards from our teens?
And when I check the way behind
I find such cherished messages from you –
absurd cuttings from the paper and cards
teasing or reassuring of laughter in the gloom…
I find a thousand small reminders
of an ever caring heart
near to me dear to me.

The music room attendants significantly grey
who sought to quell those wicked student lusts
might wonder now at what took root
despite their admonitions.
I never guessed (did you) that Cupid's older brother
silver-haired would wave a fond salute
to friendship's sturdier form.
For the part of fifty years you've shared with me
I thank you here old friend
and give you my hand in pledge towards the next.

Salute to Poetry

The rise and fall of it
The sea wrack and hajj of it
The swamping tide of it
The startling sacred and electric truth of it
That other music inward sounding
That will save me if my ears should fail.

www.ingramcontent.com/pod-product-compliance
Lightning Source LLC
Chambersburg PA
CBHW071034080526
44587CB00015B/2608